Animal Body Coverings

Why Do Owls and Other Birds Have Feathers?

Holly Beaumont

heinemann
raintree

© 2016 Heinemann-Raintree
an imprint of Capstone Global Library, LLC
Chicago, Illinois

To contact Capstone Global Library please call 800-747-4992, or visit our web site www.capstonepub.com

Edited by Clare Lewis and Kristen Mohn
Designed by Richard Parker
Picture research by Svetlana Zhurkin
Production by Victoria Fitzgerald
Originated by Capstone Global Library

Library of Congress Cataloging-in-Publication Data
Beaumont, Holly, author.
 Why do owls and other birds have feathers? / Holly Beaumont.
   pages cm.—(Animal body coverings)
 Summary: "Find out all about feathers and how they help owls fly, keep warm, hunt and survive. Discover how feathers are different on different birds and how they change as birds grow up."— Provided by publisher.
 Includes bibliographical references and index.
 ISBN 978-1-4846-2533-0 (hb)—ISBN 978-1-4846-2538-5 (pb)—ISBN 978-1-4846-2548-4 (ebook) 1. Feathers—Juvenile literature. 2. Birds—Juvenile literature. 3. Children's questions and answers. I. Title.
 QL697.4.B43 2015
 598.147—dc23   2015000291

This book has been officially leveled by using the F&P Text Level Gradient™ Leveling System

Acknowledgments
The author and publisher are grateful to the following for permission to reproduce copyright material:
Dreamstime: Dave M. Hunt Photography, 21, 23, Jhernan124, 13; iStockphoto: summersetretrievers, 9; Newscom: Photoshot/NHPA/Joe Blossom, 17; Shutterstock: Aliaksei Hintau, back cover (right), 16, 22 (top right), Chantal de Bruijne, 7, Critterbiz, 15, Dave Montreuil, 14, Dennis W. Donohue, 11, Erni, 8, fullempty, 4 (bottom), HHsu, 23 (rabbits), Lee319, cover (top), LesPalenik, 19, Marcin Sylwia Ciesielski, 18, 22 (bottom), 23, Mark Bridger, 5, meaofoto, 20, mlorenz, cover (bottom), monticello, 4 (top right), Oleksandr Chub, 23 (velvet), PeterVrabel, 23 (peacocks), Sorapop Udomsri, 6, 23, Steve Allen, 4 (top left), TheX, 10, 22 (top left), Tomatito, back cover (left), 12, Tracy Starr (feathers), cover and throughout

We would like to thank Michael Bright for his invaluable help in the preparation of this book.

Contents

Some words are shown in bold, **like this**. You can find them in the picture glossary on page 23.

Which Animals Have Feathers?

Birds have feathers. Birds have beaks and wings. They also lay eggs.

Different birds have different types of feathers.

Owls are birds. They have large, flat faces and big eyes.

What Are Feathers?

Feathers are made from the same **material** as your skin, hair, and fingernails.

Feathers grow out of the skin of birds.

Feathers can be soft and fluffy.
They can be strong and straight.

Different feathers do different jobs.

Do Feathers Keep Birds Warm?

Feathers protect birds from chilly nights and cold winters.

Birds fluff up their feathers to trap air against their skin. This air warms up and keeps the birds warm.

This great-horned owl has lots of thick feathers.

They help it to stay warm at night.

How Do Feathers Help Birds Fly?

Most birds use their feathers to help them fly.

Strong wing feathers help birds take off and fly through the air. Long tail feathers help them to steer.

wing feathers

tail feathers

Owl feathers are soft and **velvety**.

They help owls to fly quietly as they hunt for food.

Do Feathers Keep Birds Dry?

Some waterbirds, such as ducks and gulls, have very waterproof feathers.

They stop the birds from getting too wet and cold.

Owls do not like flying in the rain.
Their feathers are not very waterproof.

They get soggy and heavy. This makes
flying hard work.

Do Feathers Help Birds Hide?

Some birds use their feathers to hide from **predators**.

This nightjar nests on the ground. Its brown feathers make it hard to see.

This snowy owl is getting ready to pounce on its **prey**.

Its white feathers make it hard to spot against the snow.

What Else Are Feathers For?

Some birds don't want to hide.

For male birds, bright feathers are a good way to get noticed.

This peacock is hoping to attract a **mate** with his colorful display.

Female birds are often less colorful.

This peahen needs to stay hidden while she cares for her eggs.

How Do Feathers Change as Birds Get Older?

Many baby birds can't fly right away.

They spend their first weeks in the nest. Their soft, **downy** feathers help to keep them warm.

The young birds' wing muscles get stronger. The birds grow long flight feathers.

Soon they are ready to leave the nest and fly for the first time.

How Do Birds Take Care of Their Feathers?

Pests such as lice can eat and damage bird feathers. This can make the bird sick.

Feathers are very important to birds. They have to take care of them.

This owl is **preening**.

It is using its beak to clean its feathers. It checks the feathers for any damage.

Feathers Quiz

Which of these feathers are for keeping birds warm?

B

A

C

Answer: C

Picture Glossary

down   soft, fluffy feathers covering baby birds

mate   male and female partners that come together to make babies

material   substance from which something is made

predator   animal that hunts and eats other animals

preen   to clean and smooth feathers with a beak

prey   animal that is hunted and eaten by another animal

velvety   feeling like velvet fabric, soft to the touch

Find Out More

Web sites

Facthound offers a safe, fun way to find Internet sites related to this book. All of the sites on Facthound have been researched by our staff.

Here's all you do:

Visit *www.facthound.com*

Type in this code: 9781484625330

Books

Bodden, Valerie. *Owls* (Amazing Animals). Mankato, Minn.: Creative, 2014.

Bone, Emily. *Owls* (Usborne Beginners). New York: Scholastic, 2014

Whitehouse, Patricia. *Barn Owls* (What's Awake?). Chicago: Heinemann Library, 2010.

Index